FAMOUS BIBLE PEOPLE

HEROINES

WITH FOLD·OUT PAGES

Written by Daryl Lucas
Illustrated by Robert C. Durham

Tyndale House Publishers, Inc.
Wheaton, Illinois

SARAH

Sarah worked and worked the dough. She was making bread for her guests. They were outside with Abraham, her husband.

"Where is Sarah?" the visitors asked.

"Inside the tent," said Abraham. Sarah smiled.

"I will come back next year," one visitor said. "When I do, your wife will have a son."

Sarah dropped her dough. *A baby!* she thought, laughing quietly. *We can't have a baby! I am 90 years old. Abraham is 100. They must be joking!*

"Why did Sarah laugh?" said one visitor. "Nothing is too hard for God."

Sarah grew frightened. She did not know they heard her. "I did not laugh," she said through the tent.

"Yes, you did," said the man.

Sarah didn't say a word. A baby? At her age? But how?

REBEKAH

Rebekah went out to the well. "Hello," she said to the stranger standing there.

"Hello," he replied. The man had several helpers. He had ten camels and lots of baggage. "May I have some water?" he asked.

"Certainly," said Rebekah. "I'll get some for your camels, too." Rebekah drew jar after jar of water. The man just watched her. *Who is he?* she wondered.

"I would like to meet your family," he said.

Rebekah led him to her home. Her family greeted the man warmly.

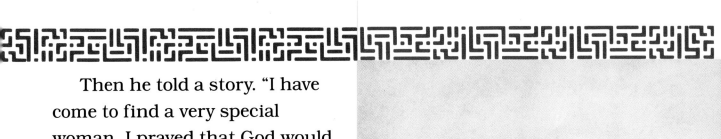

Then he told a story. "I have come to find a very special woman. I prayed that God would help me find her by showing me a sign. When I asked Rebekah for a drink, she gave all my camels a drink, too. What hard work! That was God's sign to me. She is the one I came for."

Rebekah's heart beat fast. What did he mean? Was he going to take her someplace?

RAHAB

Rahab and her family huddled together inside their small house. They heard the Israelite army marching outside. Rahab's family was frightened. "Don't be afraid," Rahab said. "When I helped the Israelite men, they promised we would be safe."

Suddenly they heard a loud trumpet blast. They heard a mighty shout. The walls of their house began to shake. The walls of the city began to fall! All around them buildings collapsed. People ran around in fright. Rahab and her family wanted to

run, too. But they stayed inside.

The noise and crumbling soon stopped. Rahab looked out the window. Through the dust, she saw nothing but ruins. The whole city had collapsed! Only her house was standing.

Rahab watched as the Israelite army rushed in. Would they remember their promise to help Rahab?

ABIGAIL

Abigail was frightened as she walked up to David, the famous warrior. She knelt down in front of him. "Please, sir," she said, "put all the blame on me. Don't hurt my family or servants. My husband didn't mean to insult you. He says bad things without thinking."

Abigail knew David was angry. Her husband had been very mean to David's soldiers. David had vowed to kill her family and servants.

"I have brought food for all your men," she continued. "Please accept these gifts and go home. Have mercy on us. God will surely bless you if you do."

Abigail waited. Would he accept her gifts and go home? Or would he keep his vow?

David stared at her angrily.

JAEL

General Sisera ran toward Jael's tent. "I will be safe there," he said to himself. "Heber and his wife, Jael, are my friends."

Jael greeted him. "Hello, friend!" she said warmly. "We heard that your army fought God's people and lost. Hurry, come hide in my tent."

Sisera sighed with relief. "Thank you," he said. He was so thirsty that he asked for water. Jael gave her guest some fresh milk.

Sisera drank it down. "General Barak, my enemy, is not far behind," he continued. "When he comes, tell him you haven't seen me."

Sisera smiled as he lay down to rest. Barak would soon come looking for him. *But thanks to Jael,* Sisera thought, *I am safe. No one can hurt me now.*

MARY MAGDALENE

"Oh no!" Mary shrieked.

"Someone took away the body!" the others gasped. Jesus had died only three days ago. Now his tomb was empty!

Mary and her friends ran home. They told Jesus' followers. Peter and John came running. But they did not know what had happened.

Mary went back to the empty tomb. She stood outside it alone, crying. Before long a man appeared. "Dear woman, what's the matter?" he said. "Who are you looking for?"

"My friend Jesus was buried here," she said. "But someone took him away. If you know where he is, please tell me. I will go get him."

Mary bit her lip. It was bad enough that Jesus was dead. She cried when they buried him the first time. Now she would have to bury him again.

Read more about these
HEROINES
in the Bible

SARAH

In the Old Testament

**Genesis 18:9-15;
21:1-7**

REBEKAH

In the Old Testament

Genesis 24:15-61

RAHAB

In the Old Testament

Joshua 6:20-25

JAEL

In the Old Testament

Judges 4:15-5:1

ABIGAIL

In the Old Testament

1 Samuel 25:23-35

MARY MAGDALENE

In the New Testament

John 20:10-16